# Minnesota

BY ANN HEINRICHS

Content Adviser: Douglass R. Anderson, Minnesota Department of Natural Resources

Reading Adviser: Dr. Linda D. Labbo, Department of Reading Education, College of Education, The University of Georgia

COMPASS POINT BOOKS ✦ MINNEAPOLIS, MINNESOTA

Compass Point Books
3722 West 50th Street, #115
Minneapolis, MN 55410

Visit Compass Point Books on the Internet at *www.compasspointbooks.com*
or e-mail your request to *custserv@compasspointbooks.com*

On the cover: Split Rock Lighthouse on Lake Superior

Photographs ©: Joseph Sohm/Corbis, cover, 1; Wally Eberhart/Visuals Unlimited, 3, 44 (middle left);
Photo Network/Karen Lawrence, 5; John Elk III, 6, 10, 12, 22, 23, 27, 28 (bottom), 32, 37, 38, 39, 43,
47; Unicorn Stock Photos/M. Silk, 7; Robert McCaw, 8, 9, 44 (top & bottom left), 45; Unicorn Stock
Photos/Phyllis Kedl, 11, 42; Richard Hamilton Smith, 13, 28 (top), 48; Charles A. Zimmerman/
Minnesota Historical Society, 15, 41; Bettmann/Corbis, 16 (top); Father Hennepin at the Falls of St.
Anthony, by Douglas Volk/Minnesota Historical Society, 16 (bottom); Fort Snelling by Henry
Lewis/Minnesota Historical Society, 17; Minnesota Historical Society, 18, 20, 21; Matthew B.
Brady/Minnesota Historical Society, 19; Unicorn Stock Photos/Andre Jenny, 24; Owen Franken/Corbis,
26, 30; AFP/Corbis, 29; Courtesy of the South Dakota State Historical Society-State Archives, 31, 46;
Phil Schermeister/Corbis, 33; Richard Hamilton Smith/Corbis, 34; David Muench/Corbis, 40; Robesus,
Inc, 43 (state flag); One Mile Up, Inc., 43 (state seal); Artville, 44 (bottom right).

Editors: E. Russell Primm, Emily J. Dolbear, and Catherine Neitge
Photo Researcher: Svetlana Zhurkina
Photo Selector: Linda S. Koutris
Designer: The Design Lab
Cartographer: XNR Productions, Inc.

**Library of Congress Cataloging-in-Publication Data**
Heinrichs, Ann.
    Minnesota / by Ann Heinrichs.
      p. cm. — (This land is your land)
    Summary: Introduces the geography, history, government, people, culture, and attractions of
Minnesota.
    Includes bibliographical references and index.
    ISBN 0-7565-0315-9
    1. Minnesota—Juvenile literature. [1. Minnesota.] I. Title. II. Series: Heinrichs, Ann. This land is
your land.
  F606.3.H45 2003
  977.6—dc21                                          2002010090

# Table of Contents

4   Welcome to Minnesota!

6   Forests, Lakes, and Prairies

15   A Trip Through Time

22   Government by the People

26   Minnesotans at Work

30   Getting to Know Minnesotans

35   Let's Explore Minnesota!


41   Important Dates

42   Glossary

42   Did You Know?

43   At a Glance

44   State Symbols

44   Making Minnesota Blueberry Crumble

45   State Song

46   Famous Minnesotans

47   Want to Know More?

48   Index

"The voice of the Great Spirit is heard in the rippling of the mighty water." This is a saying of the Dakota Sioux people. They lived in Minnesota long before European explorers arrived. The Dakota also gave Minnesota its name. They called it *Minisota*. This means "sky-tinted waters."

Minnesota's sky-blue waters ripple in thousands of rivers and lakes. Deep-green forests surround them. Lake Itasca in northern Minnesota is the source of the mighty Mississippi River.

Into this wilderness came loggers, farmers, and miners. They worked hard and lived through the fierce and snowy winters. Soon they were producing tons of lumber, wheat, and iron **ore.**

Minnesota is now a leading industrial state. Its natural beauty, however, still fills people with wonder. Come and explore Minnesota. You'll share its wonders, too!

▲ Minnesota is known for its thousands of rivers and lakes.

Head north from Minnesota, and you're in another country—Canada! Minnesota sits right at the center of the long United States–Canada border. North Dakota and South Dakota lie to the west. Iowa is on the south. Wisconsin and Lake Superior line Minnesota's eastern edge.

▲ The rocky shore of Lake Superior lies along Minnesota's eastern border.

Glaciers once covered most of Minnesota. Glaciers are massive sheets of ice. When they moved, glaciers scraped the land. Much of Minnesota became flat, with only small hills. As the glaciers melted, they dumped masses of stones, gravel, and sand. These rocky areas are called **moraines.**

Rolling **prairies** cover the southern half of Minnesota. This is the state's best farmland. In the southeast, swift streams run through deep valleys. Northeastern Minnesota was an ancient mountain range. There the glaciers ground down the mountains and left rocky, hilly land.

▲ **Minnesota's best farmland is located in the southern half of the state.**

▲ Moose roam Minnesota's many forests.

Forests cover much of Minnesota. They are home to deer, bears, moose, beavers, foxes, and raccoons. Aspen, balsam, fir, spruce, and tall pine trees grow in the northern woods. Blackberries, blueberries, and raspberries grow wild in the sunny spots there, too. Southeastern forests have deciduous trees. These are trees that shed their leaves in the fall.

Minnesota is called the Land of Ten Thousand Lakes. In fact, the state has 11,842 lakes of 10 acres (4 hectares) or more. They were created by—can you guess?—glaciers. As the glaciers moved slowly across the land, they left holes that filled with water and became lakes. The loons that nest beside those lakes are now the state bird.

▲ **The common loon is Minnesota's state bird.**

Minnesota shares Lake of the Woods with Canada. Red Lake is the largest lake that's completely within the state's borders. Lake Superior is one of North America's five Great Lakes. It is also the largest freshwater lake in the world. Duluth is an important port on Lake Superior.

▲ A view of Duluth, a port city on Lake Superior

▲ The Mississippi River begins at Lake Itasca.

The Mississippi River is Minnesota's major river. It is also the largest river in the United States. It begins as a tiny stream running out of Lake Itasca. Then it grows to become

a mighty river. Saint Paul, the state capital, and Minneapolis, the largest city, stand across the Mississippi from each other.

Many of Minnesota's rivers become waterfalls as they splash downhill. Minnehaha Falls is on Minnehaha Creek in Minneapolis. It's named after a beautiful maiden in Native American legend.

Some people joke that Minnesota has two seasons. One is "winter is coming." The other is "winter is here." Freezing weather usually begins in mid-October. Soon the snows

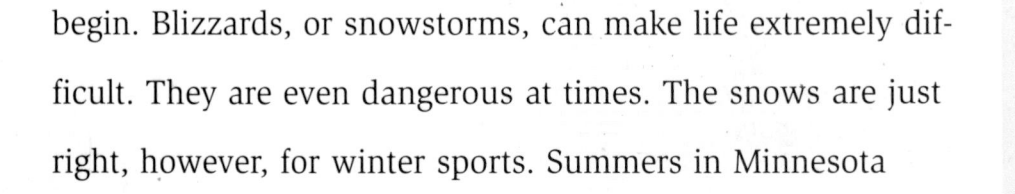

▲ **Snow is a common sight to Minnesotans.**

begin. Blizzards, or snowstorms, can make life extremely difficult. They are even dangerous at times. The snows are just right, however, for winter sports. Summers in Minnesota

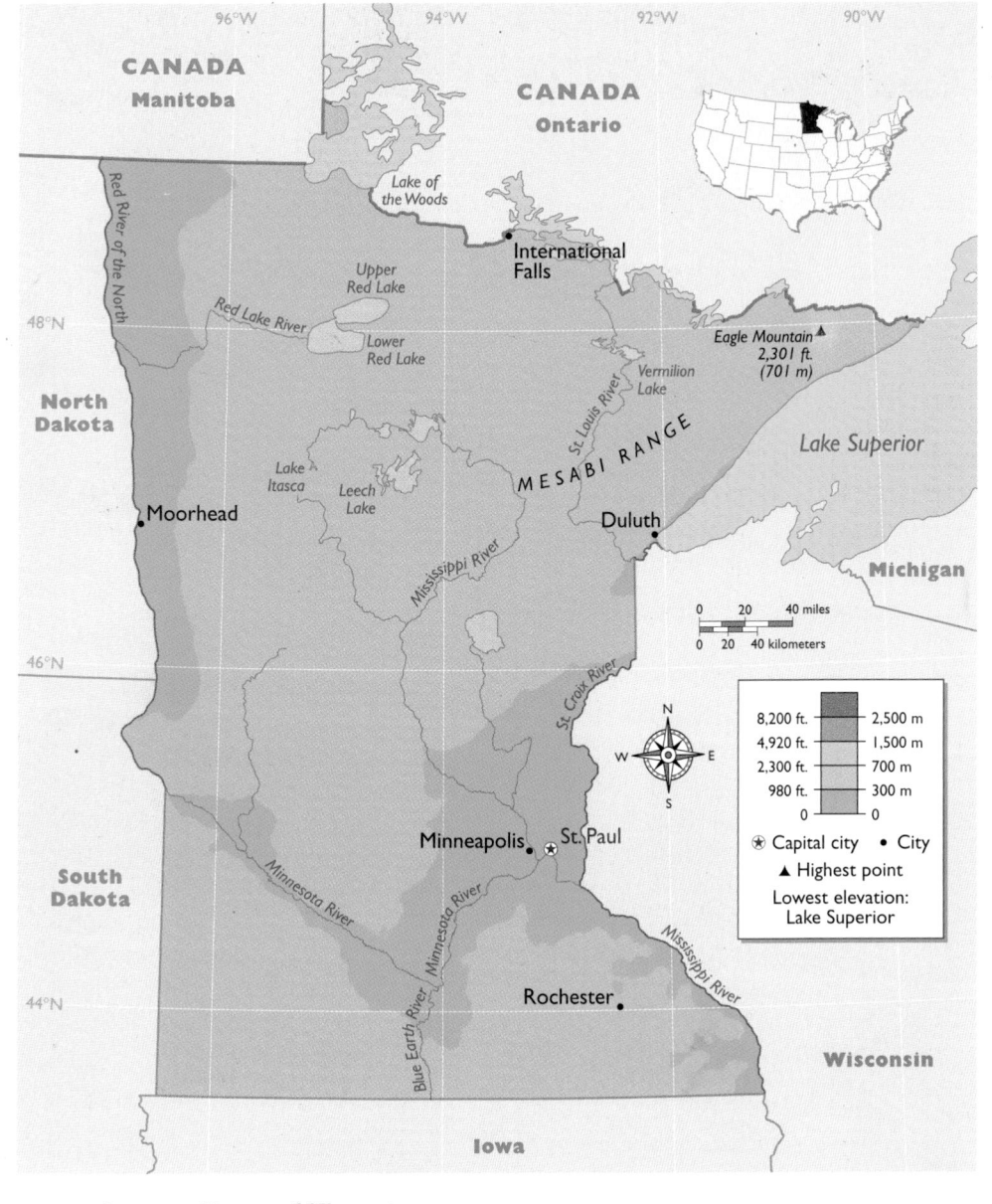

A topographic map of Minnesota

usually don't get very hot. That's the perfect time to enjoy

Minnesota's woods, rivers, and lakes.

# A Trip Through Time

Minnesota's forests once sheltered thousands of American Indians. The Dakota, one group of the Sioux, lived in the north woods. Their dome-shaped homes were covered with bark. They hunted wild animals for their food and skins. The Ojibwa (Chippewa) people began arriving in the 1600s. They drove the Dakota farther south and west.

A certain spot in southwest Minnesota was known as a **zone** of peace. People traveled hundreds of miles to get the reddish stone found at Pipestone. The Native Americans used this stone to make peace pipes.

▲ **Minnesota Indian tribes lived in wigwams, dome-shaped homes covered in bark.**

▲ French fur trader Pierre Esprit Radisson

▲ Father Hennepin and his Dakota
captors at the Falls of Saint Anthony

Two French fur traders were the first white people in Minnesota. Pierre Esprit Radisson and Médard Chouart des Groseilliers passed through northeastern Minnesota in about 1660. Daniel Greysolon, Sieur Duluth, arrived in 1679. He claimed the area for France.

The Dakota captured Father Louis Hennepin in 1680 and brought him to Minnesota. Hennepin saw waterfalls at what is now Minneapolis. He named them the Falls of Saint Anthony.

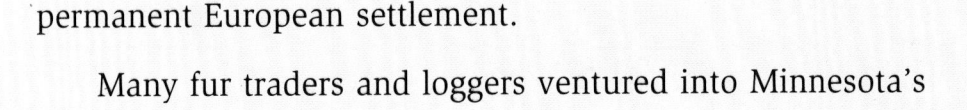

▲ **Fort Snelling was Minnesota's first permanent European settlement.**

Great Britain won eastern Minnesota from France in 1763. After the Revolutionary War (1775–1783), that land passed to the United States. Western Minnesota was added in the Louisiana Purchase of 1803. The U.S. government sent Zebulon Pike to explore this new land. Soldiers began building Fort Snelling in 1820. It became Minnesota's first permanent European settlement.

Many fur traders and loggers ventured into Minnesota's

PAUL BUNYAN "HISTORICAL" YARNS

The source of the Mississippi was no mystery to Paul, for it was one of his water wagons that sprang a leak in Itasca State Park. It hit the ground with enough force to create Lake Itasca. The overflow cut the channel for the Mississippi River.

The St. Croix River (between Wisconsin and Minnesota) came into existence, when Paul enroute to his southern camps permitted his peavey hook to drag after him.

People marvel at the irregular shapes of many northern lakes. The only explanation hot stove historians can offer is that Babe, Paul's blue ox, dug these by pawing the earth. The small nearly round lakes are his hoof prints.

Johnny Inkslinger required so much ink, In keeping Paul's books, that he had it piped to his pen with a rubber like substance made from old sour dough and spruce gum.

The winter of the blue snow was also the year of Paul's greatest griefs—he lost his shirt in the stock market, the bottom fell out of the lumber market and Babe, his blue ox, deserted him because of poor feed. He cursed the air blue—thus blue snow.

COPYRIGHT 1992 (H) A. FISHER CO., VIRGINIA, MINNESOTA

▲ **Early loggers told many tales about folklore giant Paul Bunyan.**

wilderness. The loggers told wild tales of a giant named Paul Bunyan.

Minnesota Territory was created in 1849. The U.S. government made treaties with the Native Americans. The government took over most of the American Indians' land. Soon a huge wave of new settlers arrived. In 1858, Minnesota became the thirty-second state.

Minnesotans joined the Union army in the Civil War (1861–1865). They fought bravely at the Battle of Gettysburg in 1863. Meanwhile, U.S. troops fought and defeated the Dakota back in Minnesota.

▲ **Minnesotans fought for the Union army during the Civil War.**

Thousands of **immigrants** came to farm in Minnesota. Their wheat was ground into flour at the state's many flour mills. In 1865, **prospectors** discovered iron ore in the north. By 1884, Minnesota's iron ore was being shipped to other parts of the United States. Soon the state was the leading producer of iron ore in the country.

The Great Depression of the 1930s hit Minnesota hard. Thousands of people lost their jobs. Minnesotans were a great help to the nation during World War II (1939–1945).

▲ **A Minnesota flour mill in 1900**

▲ Unemployed Minnesotans marched on City Hall in Minneapolis during the Great Depression.

Farmers raised crops to feed the troops. Also, Minnesota's iron, steel, and lumber were used to make weapons.

After the war, Minnesota's iron supply began to run low. Many new industries, however, began to grow up in the state. Millions of visitors began to arrive, too. They discovered Minnesota's deep woods and sky-blue waters. Best of all, they enjoyed Minnesota's warm and friendly people!

▲ The state capitol in Saint Paul

Saint Paul is Minnesota's capital city. It is the center of the state government. Many important government offices are in the capitol, a historic building.

Minnesota's state government is organized like the U.S. government. It is divided into three branches. They are called the executive, the legislative, and the judicial branches. With three branches, no single branch can get too powerful.

The executive branch makes sure the state's laws are carried out. Minnesota's governor heads the executive branch. Minnesotans vote to choose a governor every four years. They can keep choosing the same governor over and over, though. Voters also elect the other members of the executive branch. They include the lieutenant governor, the secretary of state, and the attorney general.

The legislative branch makes the state laws. It also decides how to spend the state's money. Voters choose lawmakers to serve in Minnesota's legislature. It has two houses, or parts—a 67-member senate and a 134-member house of representatives.

▲ This room at the state capitol is where the house of representatives meets.

Judges and courts make up the judicial branch of government. The judges know a lot about Minnesota's laws. They decide whether a person or group has broken the law. Minnesota's highest court is the state supreme court. Voters elect its seven judges.

Minnesota is divided into eighty-seven counties. Each county is governed by a group of commissioners. They collect taxes and decide how to spend the county's money. Most Minnesota cities elect a mayor and a city council. If they wish, cities may have home rule.

▲ The Hibbing courthouse is one of
several in Saint Louis County.

▲ A geopolitical map of Minnesota

Then the voters can choose the form of city government they like best.

Do you like hanging out at the mall? Then the Mall of America in Bloomington is the place for you. It's the largest shopping mall under one roof in the United States. Its floor space could cover seventy-three football fields!

▲ **Inside the Mall of America in Bloomington**

This mall is just one of Minnesota's many shopping centers. The salespeople belong to the service industry. Most Minnesota workers hold service jobs. They work in places such as stores, hospitals, schools, or banks. Medical services are very important in Minnesota. People come to Rochester's Mayo Clinic from all over the world.

Many Minnesotans work in factories. They make computers, telephones, medical equipment, and machinery. Other factory goods start out as farm products. Factories take farm-fresh crops and change them into other forms. For example, wheat becomes flour for cake mixes and cereal.

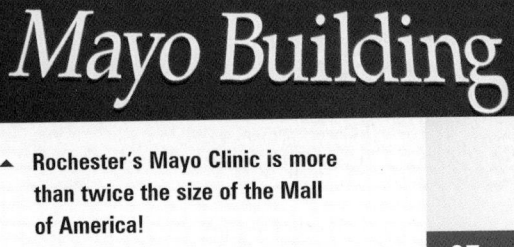

▲ Rochester's Mayo Clinic is more than twice the size of the Mall of America!

Minnesota is one of America's top ten farming states. It ranks first in the production of sugar beets, green peas, oats, and turkeys. Farms cover more than half of Minnesota's land. Hogs, dairy cattle, and beef cattle are the leading farm animals. Milk from dairy cows is made into butter and cheese. Corn and soybeans are the most important crops. Other crops are hay and wheat.

▲ Beef cattle are important farm animals.

Mining is among Minnesota's oldest industries. The Mesabi Range has the nation's largest iron-ore deposits. Most of the iron is in the form of iron oxide. It is found in a rock called taconite.

▲ The Minntac taconite plant in Mountain Iron is the largest mining facility in the United States.

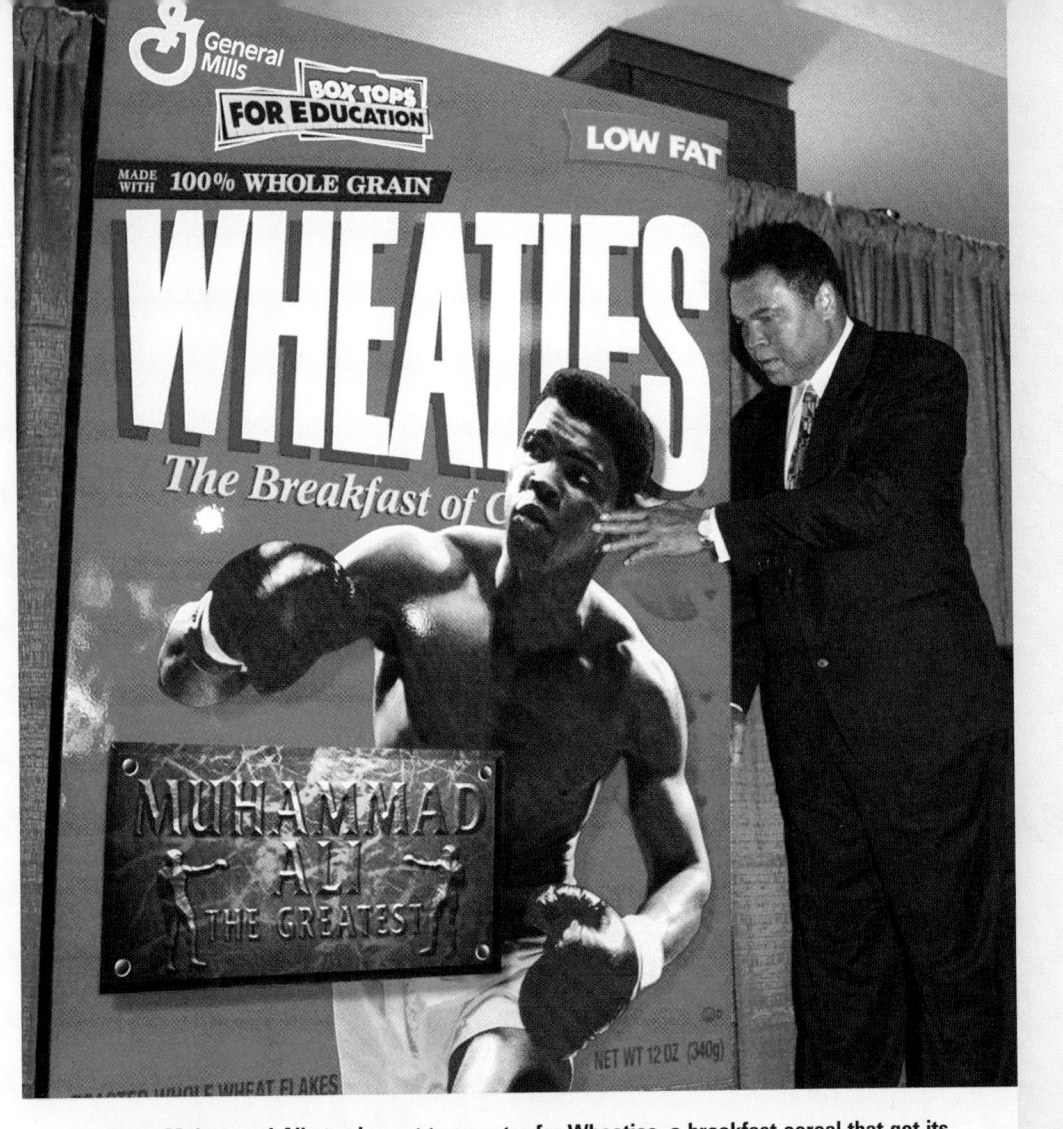

▲ Boxer Muhammad Ali stands next to a poster for Wheaties, a breakfast cereal that got its start in Minnesota.

Minnesotans gave us many firsts. They made the first pop-up toasters, snowmobiles, and staplers. We can also thank Minnesota companies for Tonka Trucks, Post-It notes, Scotch tape, microwave popcorn, and Wheaties cereal!

Minnesotans have roots in many **cultures.** French people from Canada were the earliest settlers. Others poured in from Germany, Sweden, Norway, Denmark, and Ireland. More immigrants arrived from Finland and Poland. Now African-American, Asian, and Hispanic people add to Minnesota's cultural mix.

In 2000, almost 5 million people lived in Minnesota. That made it twenty-first in population among all the states.

▲ This Asian market in Minneapolis is run by Hmong farmers, one of the many ethnic groups that live in Minnesota today.

Minneapolis is the largest city, followed by Saint Paul. The two are called the Twin Cities. More than half of all Minnesotans live in the Twin Cities area. Duluth, Rochester, and Bloomington are the next-largest cities.

Minnesotans celebrate who they are in many ways. They enjoy their **pioneer** history, **ethnic** cultures, and seasonal sports.

Ole Rölvaag wrote about Norwegian pioneers in Minnesota. Laura Ingalls Wilder wrote many children's stories about pioneer life. She recalls her childhood in Walnut Grove in *On the Banks of Plum Creek* (1937).

▲ Laura Ingalls Wilder

▲ Huge roadside statues of Paul Bunyan and Babe, the blue ox, in Bemidji

Drive through Minnesota, and you're sure to see huge roadside statues. Minnesota has about 175 of these folk-art giants. Favorite subjects are Paul Bunyan and his pet—Babe, the blue ox. You might also see a giant chicken or the Jolly Green Giant.

Many towns hold festivals to celebrate the fur-trading era. One is the Three Rivers Rendezvous in Rochester in September. Historic Fort Snelling has family-fun weekends on Memorial Day and Labor Day.

Moorhead hosts the Scandinavian Hjemkomst Festival in June. Guests enjoy the music, food, and crafts of Sweden, Norway, Finland, Denmark, and Iceland. Embarrass holds a Finnish-American Festival in June. Ethnic Days in Chisholm celebrates the area's eight ethnic groups. The Dakota people meet for **powwows** in Pipestone in July and in Mankato in September.

▲ Members of Minnesota's Indian tribes meet for annual powwows.

▲ Hot-air balloons are part of Minneapolis's Aquatennial celebration.

The biggest event of the year is the Minnesota State Fair. You can learn all about agriculture, industry, and the arts in the state of Minnesota by visiting the state fair. Saint Paul's Winter Carnival celebrates winter sports. Duluth also holds a Winter Sports Festival. In the summer, Minneapolis celebrates water sports at its Aquatennial.

Fans of professional sports in Minnesota have a lot to cheer about. Their football team—the Minnesota Vikings— has played in four Super Bowls. The Minnesota Twins won baseball's World Series twice. The Timberwolves and the Lynx are Minnesota's basketball teams. Hockey fans are wild about the Minnesota Wild.

# Let's Explore Minnesota!

Suppose it is the 1820s. You just arrived at Fort Snelling on a Mississippi steamboat. Now you're ready to take part in every-

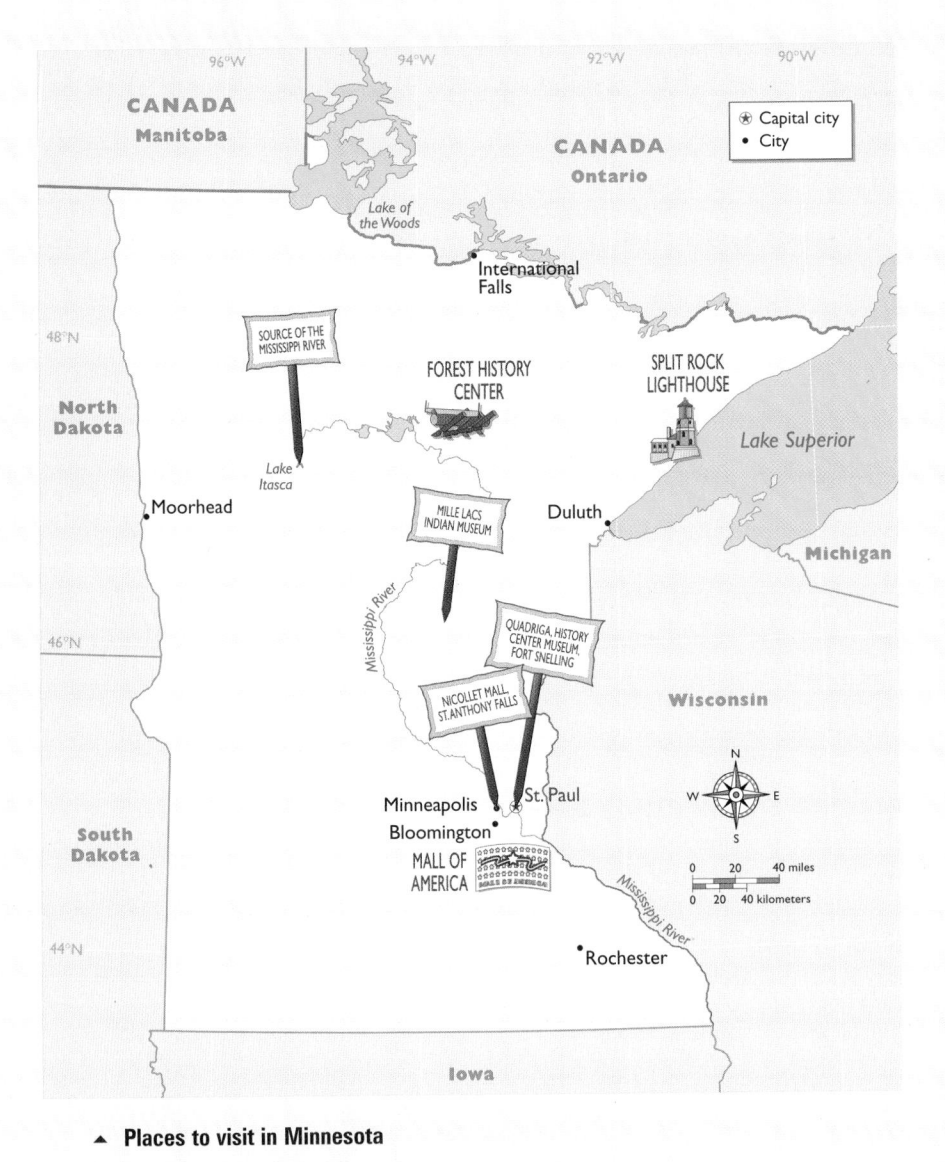

| | | |
|---|---|---|
| ⊛ | Capital city | |
| • | City | |

▲ Places to visit in Minnesota

day life. Would you like to swing a blacksmith's hammer? Scrape a hide? Mend clothes or have a cup of tea? Just join the soldiers, shopkeepers, and homemakers at this historic fort.

Logging days come to life at the Forest History Center in Grand Rapids. There you can hop aboard the *wanigan*— the floating cook's shack. It used to float downstream with the loggers.

At Split Rock Lighthouse, climb up and see a lighthouse-keeper's view. This old lighthouse stands high on a rocky bluff over Lake Superior. It beamed a warning light to ships on foggy nights.

How did the Ojibwa people cook, make beadwork, and weave birch bark? You'll discover their secrets at Mille Lacs Indian Museum in Onamia. At Pipestone, you'll learn to carve a peace pipe. For centuries, Native Americans collected pipe-stone here to make their peace pipes.

Grand Mound, near International Falls, is an ancient Indian burial site. People buried their dead here 2,000 years ago. To the east is the Boundary Waters Canoe Area. This vast wilderness has changed very little for thousands of years.

▲ Split Rock Lighthouse on Lake Superior is a popular Minnesota tourist attraction.

It's hard to miss the gleaming *Quadriga* in Saint Paul. It's a larger-than-life statue of four golden horses. They stand on the front of the historic state capitol. Inside, you can tour the capitol building and watch lawmakers in action. Then explore life in early Minnesota at Saint Paul's History Center Museum.

▲ The *Quadriga* perches below the dome of the state capitol in Saint Paul.

▲ **Saint Anthony Falls in Minneapolis**

Minneapolis lies across the Mississippi River. Its down-town Nicollet Mall covers twelve city blocks. From the mall you can travel in all directions on overhead walkways. You'll see Saint Anthony Falls from the Stone Arch Bridge. Then walk through the old flour-mill district.

▲ Lake Itasca

Just how big *was* Paul Bunyan? As big as a tall tale can get! See giant statues of Bunyan and Babe at Brainerd and Bemidji.

Near Bemidji you'll find Lake Itasca—the source of the Mississippi River. You can step across the river as it trickles out of the lake. Travel downriver, and you're in for a treat. You'll pass wild berry bushes and wild rice beds. Ducks and kingfishers live along the riverbanks, while eagles soar overhead. Maybe you'll see some busy beavers chewing sticks to make a dam.

It's easy to forget Minnesota's modern culture out here. You're happy to drift along with no sense of time. And you'll get lost in Minnesota's beauty, so ancient and so wild.

## Important Dates

**1660** Pierre Esprit Radisson and Médard Chouart des Groseilliers are the first Europeans in Minnesota.

**1783** Eastern Minnesota becomes U.S. territory.

**1803** The Louisiana Purchase adds western Minnesota to the United States.

**1820** Construction begins on the future Fort Snelling. It becomes Minnesota's first permanent European settlement.

**1849** Minnesota Territory is created by Congress.

**1858** Minnesota becomes the thirty-second state.

**1873** A three-day blizzard kills seventy people.

**1890** America's largest iron-ore deposits are discovered at the Mesabi Range.

**1894** A massive forest fire destroys Hinckley and Sandstone.

**1914** The Mayo brothers build their own medical center, known as the Mayo Clinic.

**1965** Hubert Humphrey becomes U.S. vice president under Lyndon B. Johnson.

**1977** Walter Mondale becomes U.S. vice president under Jimmy Carter.

**1987** The Minnesota Twins win the World Series.

**1991** The Minnesota Twins win the World Series again.

**1998** Former wrestler Jesse Ventura is elected governor of Minnesota.

**2002** Senator Paul Wellstone, his wife, daughter, and five others die in a plane crash in northern Minnesota.

# Glossary

**cultures**—groups of people who share beliefs, customs, and a way of life

**ethnic**—relating to a nationality or culture

**immigrants**—people who come to another country to live

**moraines**—mounds of earth and stones left by a melting glacier

**ore**—rock that contains metal

**pioneer**—someone who explores or settles in a new land

**powwows**—Native American gatherings for meetings or ceremonies

**prairies**—flat or rolling grasslands

**prospectors**—people who search for valuable minerals

**zone**—an area used for a special purpose

# Did You Know?

★ The original name of the city of Saint Paul was Pig's Eye. It was named for Pierre "Pig's Eye" Parrant, a French-Canadian trader.

★ Darwin has the world's largest ball of twine. It weighs 17,400 pounds (7,893 kg). Francis Johnson began making the ball in 1950. He worked at it for four hours a day for twenty-nine years!

★ Minnesota's Hormel Foods has made more than 5 billion cans of Spam lunch meat. Spam is short for "spiced ham."

★ It is against Minnesota law for a woman to appear on the street dressed as Santa Claus! No one enforces this old law today, though.

★ Minnesota's tallest Norway pine stands 120 feet (37 m) high in Itasca State Park.

★ Pink-and-white lady's slipper—the state flower—can live for fifty years.

★ The common loon is Minnesota's state bird. *Loon* comes from an Old Norse word meaning "wild, sad cry."

★ Minnesota has 12,000 miles (19,312 km) of snowmobile trails, more than any other state.

★ Duluth has the largest freshwater port in the world.

★ Saint Louis County is bigger than the state of Connecticut.

★ The city of International Falls is called the "Nation's Icebox." Its average January temperature is 2°F (–17°C).

★ Minnesota cows produce almost 10 billion pounds (4.5 billion kg) of milk a year.

**State capital:** Saint Paul

**State motto:** *L'Étoile du Nord* (French for "The Star of the North")

**State nickname:** Minnesota has no official nickname but many unofficial ones.

**Statehood:** May 11, 1858; thirty-second state

**Area:** 84,397 square miles (218,571 sq km); **rank:** twelfth

**Highest point:** Eagle Mountain, 2,301 feet (701 m) above sea level

**Lowest point:** Along Lake Superior, 602 feet (183 m) above sea level

**Highest recorded temperature:** 114°F (46°C) at Moorhead on July 6, 1936, and at Beardsley on July 29, 1917

**Lowest recorded temperature:** –60°F (–51°C) at Tower on February 2, 1996

**Average January temperature:** 8°F (–13°C)

**Average July temperature:** 70°F (21°C)

**Population in 2000:** 4,919,479; **rank:** twenty-first

**Largest cities in 2000:** Minneapolis (382,618), Saint Paul (287,151), Duluth (86,918), Rochester (85,806)

**Factory products:** Electronics equipment, foods, machines, printed material, paper, and wood products

**Farm products:** Milk products, soybeans, corn, beef cattle

**Mining products:** Iron ore

**State flag:** Minnesota's state flag shows the state seal on a field of blue. Around the seal is a wreath of lady's slippers, the state flower. Three dates appear on the wreath. One is 1819, the year U.S. soldiers arrived. The second is 1858, the year of Minnesota's statehood. The third is 1893, the year the flag was adopted. Nineteen stars circle the wreath. The largest star stands for Minnesota. It was the nineteenth state to join the Union after the original thirteen states.

**State seal:** The state seal shows a barefoot farmer near Saint Anthony Falls. The farmer is plowing a field near a stump. He stands for Minnesota's farming and logging industries. Nearby, a Native American on horseback represents Minnesota's first people. The state motto appears above them.

**State abbreviations:** Minn. (traditional); MN (postal)

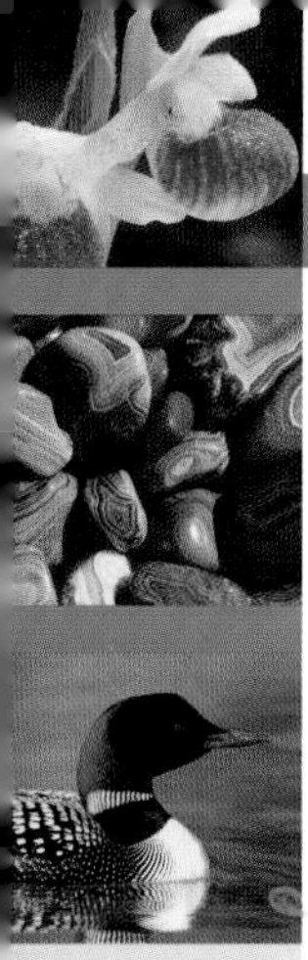

## State Symbols

**State bird:** Common loon

**State flower:** Pink-and-white lady's slipper

**State tree:** Norway pine

**State muffin:** Blueberry muffin

**State fish:** Walleye

**State mushroom:** Morel

**State grain:** Wild rice

**State gemstone:** Lake Superior agate

**State drink:** Milk

**State butterfly:** Monarch butterfly

## Making Minnesota Blueberry Crumble

Blueberries grow wild in Minnesota.

Makes six servings.

INGREDIENTS:

4 cups blueberries

3 packages instant oatmeal with
  maple and brown sugar (1.5 ounces each)

1 tablespoon sugar

3 tablespoons butter, softened

DIRECTIONS:

Preheat the oven to 375°. Mix blueberries and sugar in a 9-inch pie plate. Mix oatmeal and butter in a small bowl until it forms thick crumbs. Sprinkle the oatmeal mixture over the blueberries. Bake until it's light brown and bubbly around the edges, about 30 to 35 minutes. Serve warm. Think about being in a cozy cabin on a snowy Minnesota day! If you have a very sweet tooth, add ice cream on top.

**"Hail! Minnesota"**

*Words by Truman E. Rickard and Arthur E. Upson; music by Truman E. Rickard*

Minnesota, hail to thee!
Hail to thee, our state so dear!
Thy light shall ever be
A beacon bright and clear.
Thy sons and daughters true
Will proclaim thee near and far,
They shall guard thy fame
And adore thy name;
Thou shalt be their Northern Star.

Like the stream that bends to sea,
Like the pine that seeks the blue,
Minnesota, still for thee
Thy sons are strong and true.
From the woods and waters fair,
From the prairies waving far,
At thy call they throng
With their shout and song,
Hailing thee their Northern Star.

**Bob Dylan** (1941– ) is a singer and song-writer. "Mr. Tambourine Man" is one of his popular songs from the 1960s. He was born Robert Allen Zimmerman in Duluth and grew up in Hibbing.

**F. Scott Fitzgerald** (1896–1940) wrote stories about America's Jazz Age—the 1920s. *The Great Gatsby* (1925) is one of his most famous novels.

**Judy Garland** (1922–1969) was a singer and actress. She played Dorothy in the movie *The Wizard of Oz* (1939). Her most famous song is "Over the Rainbow."

**Hubert Humphrey** (1911–1978) was the U.S. vice president under President Lyndon Johnson (1965–1969). Before that, he was mayor of Minneapolis and a U.S. senator.

**Garrison Keillor** (1942– ) is the host of the radio show *A Prairie Home Companion,* based in a make-believe Minnesota town called Lake Wobegon.

**Sinclair Lewis** (1885–1951) was an author whose novels attacked the weaknesses he saw in U.S. society. In 1930, he became the first American to win the Nobel Prize for literature.

**Maud Hart Lovelace** (1892–1980) wrote the popular Betsy-Tacy series of books for children. The books were based on her life growing up in Mankato.

**Charles Mayo** (1865–1939) and **William Mayo** (1861–1939) were doctors who established the Mayo Clinic in Rochester. The clinic has aided millions of patients since 1907.

**Walter Mondale** (1928– ) was the U.S. vice president under President Jimmy Carter (1977–1981). Mondale ran for president in 1984 but lost. His running mate was Geraldine Ferraro, the first woman chosen as a vice-presidential candidate.

**Prince Rogers Nelson** (1958– ) is a rock music star. He is known as "Prince."

**John Pillsbury** (1828–1901) helped start his family's baking-goods company. He was Minnesota's governor from 1876 to 1882.

**Winona Ryder** (1971– ) is an actress. She appeared in her first movie at age fourteen and has been nominated for two Academy Awards. She was named after her birthplace—Winona.

**Jesse Ventura** (1951– ) has been a professional wrestler, actor, and talk-show host. His election as governor of Minnesota in 1998 caught the attention of the whole nation.

**Laura Ingalls Wilder** (1867–1957) wrote *Little House on the Prairie* (1935) and many other books about pioneer life. *On the Banks of Plum Creek* (1937) is based on her life in Walnut Grove. Wilder (pictured above left) was born in Wisconsin.

## At the Library

Baker, Sanna Anderson, and Bill Farnsworth. *Mississippi Going North*. Morton Grove, Ill.: Albert Whitman & Co., 1996.

Duey, Kathleen. *Survival! Forest Fire, Minnesota, 1894.* New York: Aladdin Paperbacks, 1999.

Fradin, Dennis Brindell. *Minnesota*. Danbury, Conn.: Children's Press, 1995.

Joseph, Paul. *Minnesota*. Edina, Minn.: Abdo & Daughters, 1998.

Shaw, Janet, and Renée Graef. *Changes for Kirsten: A Winter Story.* Middleton, Wis.: Pleasant Company, 1991.

Wilder, Laura Ingalls. *On the Banks of Plum Creek*. New York: HarperCollins, 1937.

## On the Web
### North Star
*http://www.state.mn.us*
To visit the state web site, with information on Minnesota's history, government, economy, and land

### Explore Minnesota
*http://www.exploreminnesota.com*
For a look at Minnesota's events, activities, and sights

### Minnesota Creature of the Month
*http://www.pca.state.mn.us/kids/creature.html*
To learn about a different Minnesota creature every month

## Through the Mail
### Minnesota Office of Tourism
100 Metro Square
121 Seventh Place East
Saint Paul, MN 55101
For information on travel and interesting sights in Minnesota

### Department of Economic Security
390 North Robert Street
Saint Paul, MN 55101
For information on Minnesota's economy

## On the Road
### Minnesota State Capitol
75 Constitution Avenue
Saint Paul, MN 55155
651/296-2881
To visit the state capitol

### Minnesota History Center Museum
345 West Kellogg Boulevard
Saint Paul, MN 55102
651/296-6126
To learn about Minnesota's history

# Index

American Indians. *See* Native Americans.
animal life, 8, 40
Aquatennial, 34
art, 32, 34, 38

Battle of Gettysburg, 19
Bloomington, 26, 31
borders, 6
Boundary Waters Canoe Area, 36
Bunyan, Paul, 18, 32, 40

Civil War, 19
climate, 12–14
cultures, 30, 31, 33

dairy farming, 28
Dakota Sioux tribe, 4, 15, 16, 19, 33
Duluth, 10, 31, 34
Duluth, Daniel Greysolon, Sieur, 16

Ethnic Days, 33
executive branch of government, 22–23

Falls of Saint Anthony, 16
farming, 4, 7, 20, 21, 27, 28
folk art, 32, 40
Forest History Center, 36
forests, 8, 15
Fort Snelling, 17, 32, 35–36
France, 16, 17
fur trade, 16, 17–18, 32

glaciers, 7, 9
Grand Mound, 36
Grand Rapids, 36
Great Britain, 17
Great Depression, 20
des Groseilliers, Médard Chouart, 16

Hennepin, Fr. Louis, 16
History Center Museum, 38
Hjernkornst Festival, 33
home rule, 24–25

industry, 4
iron mining, 20, 21, 28

judicial branch of government, 22, 24

Lake Itasca, 4, 11, 40
Lake of the Woods, 10
Lake Superior, 6, 10, 36
lakes, 9, 10
legislative branch of government, 22, 23
literature, 31
local government, 24–25. *See also* state government.
loon (state bird), 9
Louisiana Purchase, 17

Mall of America, 26
manufacturing, 21, 27, 29
Mayo Clinic, 27
Mesabi Range, 28
Mille Lacs Indian Museum, 36

mining, 4, 20, 28
Minneapolis, 12, 31, 34, 39
Minnehaha Falls, 12
Minnesota Lynx (basketball team), 34
Minnesota State Fair, 34
Minnesota Territory, 18
Minnesota Timberwolves (basketball team), 34
Minnesota Twins (baseball team), 34
Minnesota Vikings (football team), 34
Minnesota Wild (hockey team), 34
Mississippi River, 4, 11–12, 39, 40
moraines, 7

Native Americans, 15, 16, 18, 33, 36
Nicollet Mall, 39

Ojibwa tribe, 15, 36
*On the Banks of Plum Creek* (Laura Ingalls Wilder), 31

Pike, Zebulon, 17
pipestone, 15, 33, 36
plant life, 8, 40
population, 30
powwows, 33
prairies, 7

*Quadigra* (statue), 38

Radisson, Pierre Esprit, 16

Red Lake, 10
Revolutionary War, 17
rivers, 4, 11–12, 39, 40
Rochester, 27, 31, 32
Rölvaag, Ole, 31

Saint Anthony Falls, 39
Saint Paul, 12, 22, 31, 34, 38
service industries, 27
Split Rock Lighthouse, 36
sports, 34
state bird (loon), 9
state capital, 12, 22, 31, 34, 38
state capitol building, 22, 38
state government, 22–24. *See also* local government
statehood, 18
Stone Arch Bridge, 39

taconite, 28
Three Rivers Rendezvous, 32
timber industry, 4, 17–18, 36
tourism, 21
Twin Cities. *See* Minneapolis; Saint Paul.

waterfalls, 12, 16, 39
Wilder, Laura Ingalls, 31
Winter Carnival, 34
Winter Sports Festival, 34
World War II, 20–21

## About the Author

**Ann Heinrichs** grew up in Fort Smith, Arkansas, and lives in Chicago. She is the author of more than eighty books for children and young adults on Asian, African, and U.S. history and culture. Ann has also written numerous newspaper, magazine, and encyclopedia articles. She is an award-winning martial artist, specializing in t'ai chi empty-hand and sword forms.

Ann has traveled widely throughout the United States, Africa, Asia, and the Middle East. In exploring each state for this series, she rediscovered the people, history, and resources that make this a great land, as well as the concerns we share with people around the world.